Harriet Elizabeth Prescott Spofford

In Titian's Garden and Other Poems

Harriet Elizabeth Prescott Spofford

In Titian's Garden and Other Poems

ISBN/EAN: 9783337083274

Printed in Europe, USA, Canada, Australia, Japan

Cover: Foto ©Thomas Meinert / pixelio.de

More available books at **www.hansebooks.com**

IN TITIAN'S GARDEN

IN
TITIAN'S GARDEN
AND OTHER POEMS

HARRIET PRESCOTT SPOFFORD

BOSTON
COPELAND AND DAY
MDCCCXCVII

Thanks are due for courtesy of republication to the Messrs. Harper, Messrs. Charles Scribner's Sons, Messrs. J. B. Lippincott and Company, Messrs. Houghton, Mifflin, and Company, Mr. John Brisben Walker, the Century Company, the publishers of the Independent, the Congregationalist, and others.

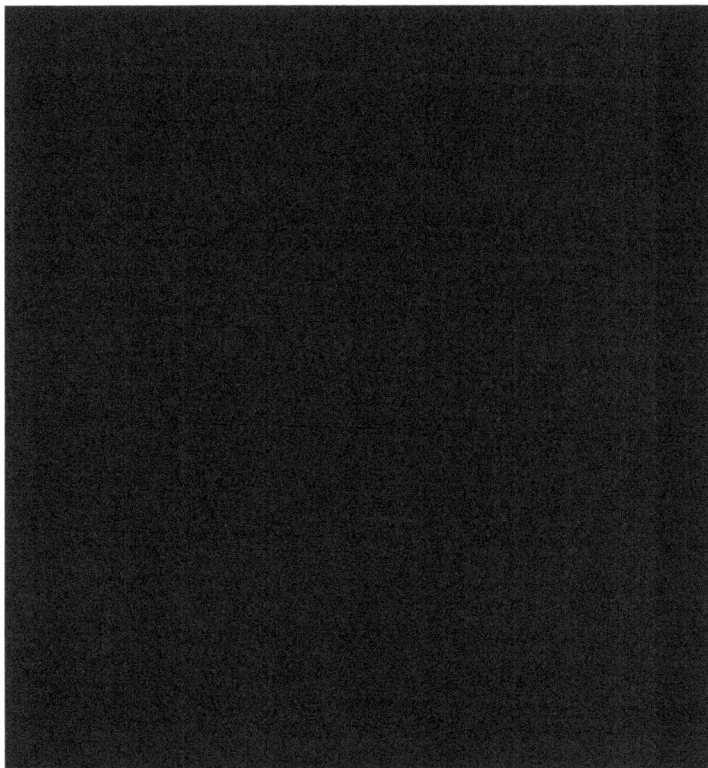

Though suns between us swing
   And æons roll,
Ever to thee I sing,
   Star of my soul!

Only to name thee now,
   In joy or dole,
Is singing's self, O thou
   Song of my soul!

CONTENTS

CONTENTS

IN TITIAN'S GARDEN

IN TITIAN'S GARDEN

WHERE the sea with drowsy murmur
    Laps the marble, and full rosy,
Far withdrawn in purple heavens,
Slopes of snow and horns of silver
Figure shining forms that slowly
Swim like giants flushed with sunset,
Cloudy swells from deeps of twilight
Round them tossing, lies the garden
Where the Master takes his pleasure
When the pencil leaves his fingers
Tingling still with magic cunning, —
While from dome and campanile
Wandering winds bring airy music,
Showers of bell-tones lightly falling
As the dusk falls, half caressing,
Tenderly like some soft mantle
Folding him in starry shadows.

Still within the spell of daydreams,
Stepping stately down the stairway,
Like some great doge of his painting
Sweeping out of frame and panel,
Moves the Master.　And the jasmines

Blow their breath forth to salute him,
Lemon leaves with piercing sweetness
Touch and whisper, laurels rustle,
Cleaving from the carven satyr
Towards him turns the passion-flower.
All the garden glooms and glitters,
Wine-dark cup and pearly petal,
Every deepest dye revealing
Hid in inmost cell and tissue
To the eye that searches sunlight,
Lord of color that is nameless,
Shut within the ray's recesses
For a further finer vision.

Here he sups with Sansovino,
With Zuccato, scheming, seeing
For San Marco the new marvel
Growing like a golden bubble
Poised in happy air above them.
Here the merry Aretino
Breaks the flask and takes the creaming,
Makes them jests and sings them sonnets.
And some girl sea-bronzed and sparkling,
On her cheek the stain ensanguined,
Bears aloft the bossy salver :
As the innocent Lavinia
Brought them in old days of revel
Fruits and flowers amesh with sunbeams, —
No red burnish of pomegranates,
No cleft peach in velvet vermeil,
No bright grapes their blue bloom bursting,

6

IN TITIAN'S GARDEN

Dews between the cool globes slipping,
Dews like drops of clouded sapphire,
But the brighter self and spirit
Glowed illusive in her beauty !

Out of spheres of golden nightfall,
Melting skies in melting currents,
All along the festive evening
Come the rout to Casa Grande,
Contarini and Cornaros,
Zios, Dannas, gay and gallant,
Many a proud Venetian noble
Sword on hip and chain on shoulder,
Splendid in his cap and jewel —
Black the Ten, in awful presence
All unguessed, behind him, flashing
From his pleasure to his prison,
When the torches quench them quickly
And the water-way is narrow
Where the treacherous palace-shadow
Cuts the moonlight like a sword-blade.
One great joy, a glorious phantom,
One great memory, following after,
Red with rapture, trembling, smiling,
Bringing all of life to blossom,
Worth the dungeon, worth the dagger !

Lute-strings tinkling, voices warbling,
Stealing over gilded waters,
Mother o' pearl and shining furrows,
Float the gondolas, and flocking

IN TITIAN'S GARDEN

Like bright doves the gracious ladies
Bring their homage to the Master.
How they love him, how they serve him,
These white women, hair all golden
Dropping down their snowy bosoms,
Clad in cloth of gold, and shedding
Laughter as they move about him !
O'er the wall the roses clamber,
Vagrant sprays and torn corollas
That the bee has robbed beforetime,
Telling of the lovely joyance
With the man of ninety summers, —
Every one of all those summers
Like wide-spreading flowers that open
Prodigal their silken curtains,
Each one fuller than the last one
Of the perfume and the honey,
Of the wine of life unwasted.

Slowly as a dream fades, waking,
Fades the flush along the summits,
And in shoreless floods the moonlight
Washes all the sky in silver,
Washes all the emerald shallows,
Lifts in light the dim barge drifting
To the dark of San Michele.
Far away a voice is ringing,
Sweetness lurking in the echo,
Like the waft of love forgotten,
On a wind from nowhere blowing,
When one passes bearing myrtles.

8

IN TITIAN'S GARDEN

So death comes to Venice,
  The city of dreams,
We know that hearts ache there,
  They break there it seems.

Love burns like the rose there,
  And falls like its leaf,
And balsams and balms there
  Distil out of grief.

Bear they the dead there,
  Or bear they the bride,
Splendor floats with them
  Along the dark tide.

By noonlight, by moonlight,
  By dawnlight's soft hours,
When death comes to Venice
  They hide it in flowers.

Dies the tune and dies the echo,
Dies the moon's bloom like remembrance
Falling from supernal spaces.
Gone the lover and the lady,
Fled is all the frolic pageant
Fleeting moth-like down the ripple,
Vanishing as sparks skim widely,
Lost at last in starry distance.
Left alone, the mighty Master, —
Who has honor of all people,
Fishing-men along Guidecca,
Dogaressa, and donzella,

9

Who has pope to friend, and princes,
Pomp and power before him waiting,
Earth with nothing to surrender, —
Feels the world of thronging silence,
Beckons the unseen about him,
Dreams his dreams and calls his phantasms.
Once again fair Violante
Leads him through a land enchanted.
Once again his wife Cecilia
In her smiling holds all heaven.
Was't of old, or was't this morning,
Violet mists along Cadore,
Almonds shaking in the sunshine
Twinkling webs of dewy sparkles,
Made the day a glory ?
                                    Softly
Depth on depth the summer shadows
Open hollow after hollow,
Bare a ruddy heart and give him
Marrow of strange tinct and secret.
Overhead in fragrant darkness
Drooping boughs are bending, brooding,
Winds are murmuring, waters slipping,
And a nightingale remotely
Sets a sigh to singing.
                                    Clearly
All the joy of lovely living,
Lust of the eyes, and earth's wide wonder,
Pride of life and bounding heart's blood,
Are his birthright and possession,
Beauty, the surcharge of Godhead,

10

IN TITIAN'S GARDEN

Brimming like the sea and swelling
For his element and being,—
He, whose many years confirm him
That the empurpled dust had taken,
Were it something less than precious,
Primal shape and sumptuous seeming
In no thought divine, and compassed
No informing fire of heaven.
Listen — all about him flowing —
Is it but a fond remembering ?
Melodies and voices mingling,
Voices flashing on his fancy
Wild white swans their wet wings beating
Far in sounding Istrian channels.
Who are these, old numbers trolling
Once he sang in his own heyday?
Stars above in pallid places,
Stars in tranquil tides below them,
What young monk his grate regretting,
What mad poet drunk with dreaming,
Where the wide lagoon goes darkly,
And the night feels morning quicken !

Build up, build up the mountain walls,
    The gleaming gorges thick with mist,
The crags through veiling waterfalls
    Sun-smitten into amethyst !

Bring from the far and outer verge,
    With perfume on long breezes curled,
Beauty, that deathless Demiurge
    Through whom the Maker made the world!

IN TITIAN'S GARDEN

Bring music of the winding horn,
    And airy shapes of tender things,
And keep the place where Love is born,
    And starts and shakes his purple wings !

Answering tones from further outposts,
Does he dream them — does he hear them ?
Finer thrills of fainting music
Down full-throated bells recurrent,
In a sea of silver clangor,
Throbbing far on tides of morning
Through the dark rich prime, and swimming
To the measure of his pulses, —
Some high spirit bathed in heaven,
Shrilling his imperious gladness,
Seeing Venice on her waters
Like the towers of that fair city
The apocalyptic herald
Saw, more luminous than daybreak,
Hanging in the empyrean.

    In the dew and the dark and the coolness
        I bend to the beaker and sip,
    For the earth is the Lord's, and its fulness
        Is held like the cup to my lip.

    For his are the vast opulences
        Of color, of line, and of flight,
    And his was the joy of the senses
        Before I was born to delight.

IN TITIAN'S GARDEN

Forever the loveliness lingers,
  Or in flesh, or in spirit, or dream,
For it swept from the touch of his fingers
  While his garments trailed by in the gleam.

When the dusk and the dawn in slow union
  Bring beauty to bead at the brim,
I take, 't is the cup of communion,
  I drink, and I drink it with Him !

THE VIOLIN

Viva fui in sylvis,
Dum vixi tacui,
Mortua dulce cano.

ALL the leaves were rustling in the forest,
All the springs were bubbling in the moss ;
What light laughter where the brooks were spilling,
What lament I heard the branches toss,
Ah, what pipings gave me thrill on thrill !
All the world was wild with broken music —
I alone was silent, I was still.

White the moonbeam wove its weird about me,
Starshine clad my boughs with streaming flame,
Mighty winds caressed me out of heaven,
Storm-clouds in a fleece upon me came,
Earth's deep juices fed me all my fill —
Strains swept through me fit for sovran singing —
I, alas, was silent, I was still.

I was still, though callow buds were swarming,
Still, though sylvan life throughout me stirred.
Embassy though mine of praise and passion,
Melancholy waiting on my word,
Inarticulate those murmurs stole!
What without the rhythmic thrall were transport?
What were longing ?   Silent was the soul.

When the sleeting rains fled far on tempest,
With the eyry rocking under me,
Part of the great planet flying northward,

14

THE VIOLIN

Star among the stars I fain would be.
    Wide upon the gale I spread my plume —
Oh, not mine to burst in clamorous chanting,
    Syllabling some eager song of doom !

I remember me of gladsome mornings
    Where the sun swept in a quickening flash
Down long lanes to pass in glooms of verdure,
    While it gave my stem a golden plash.
    Happy outcry made the hollows ring.
I had sung then with the singing children —
    Woe is me, there was no voice to sing.

I remember me of summer twilights —
    Red the brand burned in the smouldering west,
While two lovers leaned on me together,
    And I felt their tremor through my breast.
    Softly, softly sighed the lonely thrush
Till the heart swooned in a joy of sorrow —
    I could only listen through the hush.

When the wanderer spent his soul with weeping
    Deep in the long bracken at my base,
Low my shade bent round him as a covert,
    Wearying to whisper words of grace.
    Bitterly with grief acquainted then
All his sadness passed into my being,
    Sadness that would never forth again.

Came the woodsman with his stroke and felled me ;
    Strong suns sucked the life from every cell ;
Bending, purfling, hearing unsung warbles,

Came the craftsman with his cunning spell,
Gave me flowing lines beloved of men.
As old kings in strange gums swathed and vested
I lay dead.   What mattered singing then?

Came the Master — drew his hand across me —
Oh, what shocked me, what great throb of bliss
Wakened me to pulse on pulse of rapture —
Soul my soul, I never dreamed of this!
Breath of horn and silver fret of flute,
Compass of all nature's various voices,
I was singing — I who once was mute!

Winding waters, silken breezes blowing,
Fragrances of morning, filled my tune,
Glimpses of the land where dreams are mantled,
East o' the sun and rearward of the moon,
Songs from music's ever-swelling tide,
Music beating up the walls of heaven —
I had never sung had I not died!

TRUMPETS IN LOHENGRIN

HARK! 'T is the golden trumpets of the dawn
Sounding the day!
Music, O Music fain!
From rosy reaches drawn,
And fall of silver rain,
Along the call how swift the sunrise streams!
Sound, sound again,
O magical refrain!

16

Peal on peal winding through the dewy air,
Peal on peal answering far off and fair,
Peal on peal bursting in victorious blare !
  Sound, sound again,
  With your delicious pain,
  O wild sweet haunting strain,
Till the sky swell with hint of heavenly gleams
And the heart break with gladness loosed from
  dreams !

What buoyant spirit breathes the breath of morn
And earth's delight,
  Trumpets, O trumpets blest !
   Great voices, born
  Of consecrated gest,
Across the ramparts ring and faint and fail !
  O echoes, pressed
  On some ethereal quest,
Touch all the joyance to a tearful dew,
With melancholy gathering o'er the blue —
Infinite hope, infinite sorrow, too !
  And, heard, or guessed,
  Sweet, sweet, O sweet and best,
  Fall'n from some skyey crest,
O horns of heaven, give your hero hail,
Blown to him from the Kingdom of the Grail !

THE FLIGHT

WHEN the great ice comes down on the river,
   With the roar of a mighty voice abroad,
Crying, " Deliver! O shores, deliver ! "
The giant pines of the island shiver,
The rooted rocks of the mid-earth quiver,
   Hearing and fearing the tread of a god.

" Come," sung the Sea, " O breath of my being,
   Drawn from me, drawn from me, summer days
      long !
Hill-tarn and cavern too sombre for seeing,
You that have swung in the sun shall be fleeing ;
Now my winds blow, my tides press to your
      freeing,
   Urging and surging and filled with my song! "

Green in the moonbeam it lay at the singing,
   Silver with froth of a frozen foam,
Red in the sunrise its arrow-flame flinging,
Azure while over it moonlight was winging,
Dark as the midnight tide when it went springing,
   Bending and rending went springing for home.

What a great music you heard through your
      dreaming
   When in a moment the ice went free !
Wild as the Valkyr her battle-cry screaming,

With groaning and sighing, and ghostly the gleaming,
And shifting the shapes that towered shouldering
    and streaming,
  Bursting and thirsting and mad for the Sea!

THE PINES

COULDST thou, Great Fairy, give to me
   The instant's wish, that I might see
Of all the earth's that one dear sight
Known only in a dream's delight,
I would, beneath some island steep,
In some remote and sun-bright deep,
See high in heaven above me now
A palm-tree wave its rhythmic bough !

And yet this old pine's haughty crown,
Shaking its clouds of silver down,
Whispers me snatches of strange tunes
And murmur of those awful runes
Which tell by subtle spell, and power
Of secret sympathies, the hour
When far in the dark North the snow
Among great bergs begins to blow.

Nay, thou sweet South of heats and balms,
Keep all thy proud and plumy palms,
Keep all thy fragrant flowery ease,
Thy purple skies, thy purple seas !
These boughs of blessing shall not fail,

These voices singing in the gale,
The vigor of these mighty lines —
I will content me with my pines!

THE SINGING ON THE RIVER

WHEN nights are dusk and airs are soft,
  Where stars and tree boughs quiver,
How sweet beneath Deer Island's cliff
  The singing on the river!

I hear oars dip and waters lap,
  The tide turns slowly swinging,
When from the great mysterious dark
  The sudden voice comes ringing —

The sudden silver voice that far
  Its happy burden launches,
Till the weird pine at Hawkswood's Bend
  Stirs all its dewy branches.

And where the Laurels gloom it steals,
  And dies, remotely floating,
On Salisbury shore as dies the song
  Of some aerial boating.

Perchance a young girl's voice wherein
  All love and joy are clinging,
Perchance the river-gods', perchance
  The great dark's voice is singing —

The great soft tingling dark that hangs
  With warmth and flower scents freighted,
The dark that clung to Eden's slopes
  While God and Morning waited.

Ah, till the last of the clear tones
  In throbbing silence shiver,
How sweet beneath Deer Island's cliff
  That singing on the river!

SPRING MEASURES

I

APRIL WINDS

COME, little April winds,
  Puff your dear lips ;
Curl round the veering vanes,
  The waiting ships,
And toss, the forest through,
  The topmost tips !
There is no life till you
Bring back the blue.

Come, sky-born April winds,
  And blow, and blow
The fleecy cloud above,
  The drift below,

And set your breath before
  The salt sea's flow,
And on the brook's bright floor
Your jewels pour !

Come, mighty April winds,
  And bid the bud
Call to its blushing cheek
  The earth's best blood ;
On dearth of bloom, and drouth,
  Blow flowers in flood ;
Blow Summer and the South
From your sweet mouth!

II

IN THE WOOD

NOW it is April!   Come with me
  Into the heart of the waiting wood,
Dim with great emerald glooms, and sweet
  With sense of slumberous solitude.

Here in the dewy gleam alit,
  With flickering sun and fitful blue,
Down the tranced depths how strong, it seems,
  The spell is laid, how silent too!

As if the moveless hemlocks there,
  The mystic cedars, knew the bond
That held them cast in changeless calm,
  Waiting the lifting of a wand.

22

SPRING MEASURES

Nay, then, has silence' self a voice
  Of wide and murmurous music? Hark!
That distance shot with quivering light —
  You thought it mute? You thought it dark?

Where you shall tread, all unaware,
  The velvet moss, from hiding cool
A troop of sparkles toss and fly,
  A troop of dimples break the pool.

And close about the kingly bole
  In the dead bracken of his lair
A cloud of bursting buds have shed
  Their dusty sweetness on the air.

The maple like an ember burns
  Far down the misty forest reach;
Yonder the shadows prank themselves
  In the green sunshine of the beech.

And where that great bough slowly lifts
  A dusky plume, and falls on rest,
Nestles a mother-bird, and broods
  The song to come beneath her breast.

The whisper of the parting sheath,
  The pushing bud, is singing there
Under the breath to half-guessed tunes
  Of trickling waters everywhere.

With thrills along the last year's leaf,
  With seeds that start, with wings that whir,
With motion and with sound, the world,
  The dark sweet world, is all astir.

In the deep wood this April day
  Feel, then, with what a yearning flight
Through every darkling clod the earth
  Springs upward like a soul to light!

III
IN SONG TIME

I

WHEN first the blush of the sweet earth, be-
    cause the sun has turned her way,
Suffuses light and lofty skies, and hides in veils of
    rosy gray;
When winds come blowing out of heaven, faint
    with a breath of unknown bliss,
The bloom of shores the soul has known in some far
    other morn than this;
When life is gushing everywhere in pulses from
    the primal source,
And all the answering planet thrills and trembles to
    the quickening force;

When silver showers are rent in twain by sun-
    beams in their arrowy drive,
And grassing all the woody ways, the dark mould
    fain would be alive;

24

SPRING MEASURES

When down the happy orchard aisles the apple-
 trees begin to blow,
And wrap their rugged being round with brooding
 wings of blushing snow ;
When children wild with laughter snatch the firstborn violets of the year,
And smouldering, flashing, beauty breaks a flame of
 blossom far and near ;

When bees are humming, swallows darting, leaves
 are rustling, brooks foam white ;
When birds to music shake the air, and just to
 breathe is sheer delight —
Oh, then the poet feels him part of all the lovesome
 stirring thing,
Thrills, as the mighty mother thrills, to the great
 impulse of the spring,
Wild joyous motions flitter where the pool lay dark
 and silent long,
The fount of singing overflows, his soul is nothing
 but a song!

II

SAID the archangels, moving in their glory,
 Seeing the suns bend out along their courses,
 Seeing the earth swim up in vernal light,
Seeing the year renew her ancient story, —
 Ask we here the Lord of all the finer forces
 To make us now a poet whose song shall
 reach our height!

Fain would we know the impulse ever fleeing,
   Fleeing in light o'er the battlements of even,
      Fleeing in love that lifts the universe like wings ;
Fain would we know the secret of our being,
   Blush for a moment with the inmost joy of
      heaven —
      Make us then a poet whose song shall tell
      these things !

From his rosy cloud, a Voice, — O wonder !
   All my harp-strings tremble to sweet singing !
   Life, O lovely life, is at the flood !
Hear the torrents' far melodious thunder,
   Hear the winds' long sweep, the joyous thickets
      ringing,
      Forests bow and murmur, and blossoms burst
      their bud !

Israfel, the Voice, was warbling, — Follow
   Where the wild swift music winds and doubles !
   Follow ! When the sap whirls longing for the
      light,
When the first thrush thrills the dusky hollow,
   Every heart on earth with jocund spirit bubbles,
      And every soul 's a poet whose song surmounts
      our height !

IV

OUTDOORS

BLUE as the ephod robe
   Of desert story
Deepens the sky and burns
   With inner glory.
Blue, blue it burns and bears
   Upon its bosom
Branch-work of rose and snow
   And tufted blossom,
Tracery of coral stem,
   Foam-wreath of flower,
Raining from airy heights
   A silken shower.
And while full odors steal
   With soft caressing,
Out of exhaustless wells
   Forever pressing,
To gaze is transport and
   To breathe is blessing !

Sometimes I think the Lord
   Of all this splendor
Looks at it with a love
   Exceeding tender.
Because He loves it so
   It seems to capture
Some effluence divine,
   Some source of rapture,
Fusing with earth and air,
   In wondrous leaven,

IN TITIAN'S GARDEN

The beauty too intense
    Of upper heaven!
Sometimes in vision half
    The marvel seeing,
The vast, swift loveliness
    Around me fleeing
Is but a gleam, a glance,
    Of God's own being!

AFLOAT

WINDING in and out the fragrant meadow,
    Now the boatway lapses into shadow,
While the high-arched forest branches quiver
O'er green depth of sunshine in the river.
Anchored lilies dip before our gliding;
Scarlet-finned the perch below are sliding;
Here a happy nest among the sedges
Hides its pearls behind the reedy edges,
Here the blue wings of a flitting swallow
With the fluttering pennon flash and follow.

All at once the world is wider round us,
Lonely marshes far and near have bound us,
Up their creeks a glistening tide goes swimming
Where the sails like pointed flames are skimming.
Close above, the idle lighthouse towers
Like a phantom through the shining hours,
Looms along the low and barren beaches,
Over all the salty ocean reaches,
Over all the white-plumed crests that landward
Toss the fleeting foam-bow of their standard.

28

THE FIRE–FLIES IN THE WHEAT

Ah, the soaring, sinking, of our flying —
So may spirits pass who leave their dying.
What a fresh breath from the hoary hollows !
Turn again, ye little scudding swallows —
Space nor grace be found for summer's nestlings
Where these winds and waters keep their wrestlings.
Ancient winds from ancient heavens are falling,
Awful deeps to awful deeps are calling !
How the great swells of the bar are leaping
Purple-breasted, froth-flecked, to our sweeping !
Mount them, gallant bark, with gallant riding,
Music echoes in their angry chiding,
Music in the breakers' silver thunder,
Music in the billow cleft asunder !
Now no more the fitful west wind teases, —
Loose the sail !   And blow, ye mighty breezes !

THE FIRE–FLIES IN THE WHEAT

AH, never of a summer night
 Will life again be half as sweet
As in that country of delight
   Where straying, staying, with happy feet,
   We watched the fire-flies in the wheat.

Full dark and deep the starless night,
   Still throbbing with the summer heat ;
There was no ray of any light,
   But dancing, glancing, far and fleet,
   Only the fire-flies in the wheat.

In that great country of delight,
　Where youth and love the borders mete,
We paused and lingered for the sight,
　While sparkling, darkling, flashed the sheet
　Of splendid fire-flies in the wheat.

That night the earth seemed but a height
　Whereon to rest our happy feet,
Watching one moment that wide flight,
　Where lightning, brightening, mount and meet
　Those burning fire-flies in the wheat.

And still the words whose memory might
　Make an old heart with madness beat,
Whose sense no music can recite,
　That chasing, racing, rhythmic beat
　Sings out with fire-flies in the wheat.

Oh, never of such blest despite
　Dreamed I, whom fate was wont to cheat —
And like a star your face, and white —
　While mingling, tingling, wild as sleet,
　Stormed all those fire-flies through the wheat.

Though of that country of delight
　The farther bounds we shall not greet,
Still, sweet of all, that summer night,
　That maddest, gladdest night most sweet,
　Watching the fire-flies in the wheat !

MIDSUMMER

DAWN–TIDE growing, rose-light sowing,
Heaven showing bloom and sheen,
With the summer morning breaking
Silver soft and all serene,
Oh the still delight of waking
When the grass is in the mowing
And the leaf is green !

Dark kine lowing, slow mists throwing
In their going, half unseen,
Where the thatch is shine and shadow
Oh, below the sail to lean,
Barges dropping down the meadow,
When the grass is in the mowing
And the leaf is green !

Waters flowing, sunshine glowing,
Breezes blowing in between,
Every spray a blossom giving,
Every dewdrop Hippocrene,
Oh the loveliness of living
When the grass is in the mowing
And the leaf is green !

THE HUNT

WILD stream the clouds, and the fresh wind
    is singing,
  Red is the dawn, and the world white with
    rime, —
Music, O music ! The hunter's horn ringing !
  Over the hill-top the mounted men climb.

Flashing of scarlet, and glitter, and jingle,
  The deep bay, the rhythm of hoof and of
    cry,—
Echo, O echo ! The winds rush and mingle !
  Halloo, view halloo! And the Hunt has swept
    by.

Stay ! All the morning is hushed and is sober,
  Bare is the hill-top and sad as its wont, —
Out of the ghost of a long-dead October
  Blows as the dust blows the ghost of the Hunt !

OFF BRETON COAST A THOUSAND YEARS AGO

PUT the boat round, and head her for the sea !
  Did I hear, Damrosée ? Did you answer me ?
  Has the wind so sweet a sigh as that whisper
    which went by ?
Oh, bring the boat about, and head her for the sea !

32

OFF BRETON COAST

Soft the old gray towers sink beyond the view,
Clouds of wings above them dark upon the blue;
   Oh, the rooks come back at night, however long
      their flight,
But never more, Damrosée, those towers encircle
   you!

Up blaze the bonfires on the great bluff's side,
Tremblingly the bridegroom hastens to the bride:
   With many winters' snows upon his head he
      goes;
Oh, tremble, dotard, like the lights that in your
   jewels hide!

Tremble! For the tide between yourself and her
Wide swells, and wider, a purple plunderer!
   A thousand spears of light, it strikes your startled
      sight,
And every spear a foeman, and the great winds
   stir!

Many a time, Damrosée, have I sailed along the
   lea,
When nights were still and dark, and when glad
   gales were free,
   Seen your towers shine where they stand, and
      fair, I said, the blooming land, —
Oh, fair and broad! — but my dominion is the
   sea.

3

Oh, beautiful dominion, where the wild storms
    bloom,
Where field on field forever flies the foam-wreath's
    plume,
  Where sleep the silver swells, where the moon-
    light weaves her spells,
Where sunrise like a spirit bursts from the gray
    gloom!

See, how far above us the bright sail takes its
    breath !
See, how far below us the great sea darkeneth !
  Oh, Damrosée, wild the bliss, heart to heart
    and kiss to kiss,
With nothing but a tree's stem between our flight
    and death !

TWO ANTIQUES

I

THE LAMP

CLEAR as if she passed me now —
    Stepping leopard-like and quick,
Long-limbed, with a furtive grace —
I can see the ivory brow ;
See the gold bronze of the face
Burn with joy, I know not how ;
See beneath the scarf the hair
Black as midnight, fragrant, thick,

34

TWO ANTIQUES

Falling all about her there.
And as fire bursts from char,
Each eye kindle like a star !
When her long-lost lamp I bring —
There 's such magic in the thing —
From her ashes scattered far,
From her thousand years away,
She comes back to me to-day.

Just a little earthen lamp —
Here the oil swam, here the wick,
Here the flame went flaring back
If the bearer turned her quick ;
Turned her in the shadowy space,
Saw the flash of one swart face ;
Saw the eager arms, and — hark ! —
Sprang aside, and let the dark
Blow her out and drown the spark !

II

THE TEAR BOTTLE

HERE a sudden flush of flame,
And here a sheet of azure glory,
Blood-red depth, and lucid green
    Of seas a stooping storm makes hoary.
Such a blaze sheds no sweet queen,
    Jewel-eyed, by gems attended ;
No imperial pearl so fair ;
No fire-opal half so splendid.

35

Tiny treasure, making play
Of beauty out of long decay,
Gathering light in some old tomb
Through twenty centuries of gloom !

Passion of wild joy and life,
 Passion of vast death and sorrow,
Tremor of delicious hope
 Beating breathless toward to-morrow ;
Desolation and despair
 Prostrate in the dead night-hushes ;
Pallor of vague fear and dole,
 Stormy surge of love and blushes —
With disintegrating power,
In slow enchantment hour by hour,
Wrought old earth the spell ? or here
Were all these splendors in a tear ?

THE SECRET

NAY ! nay ! I have not told you yet !
 I cannot tell you while you let
Your heart shake so.   Here, lend your ear —
Ah, God in heaven, have no fear !
'T is I, not you, should quake, for lo,
This many a year I 've trembled so
When in the dead of the dark I heard
The whistle of a waking bird,
Or saw the moon with leprous stain
Look through the waiting window-pane,

36

THE SECRET

As if a ghost stood there a space
With eyes that lit the troubled place,
What time the arras on the wall
Let all its shadows rise and fall,
And strange soft rustlings swept the room,
And ghoul and goblin filled the gloom,
Appalling shapes with threatening gleams,
Till back I cowered to my dreams !

Sometimes the wind comes up and sings
Like a lost soul ; the great shield rings
Against the wainscot.   Give a glance,
The knight in armor, with his lance,
Half stirs and lifts a murderous arm ;
Icy, and curdling with alarm,
I cry out, and the echoes cry —
Oh, so I heard that voice once — I —
And the wind wails on as before
Over the wild and lonely moor.

Nay, hear me ; I must tell you now —
Damp, damp, the sweat stands on my brow,
And cold, the very cold of the grave
Creeps up.   Help ! help me, you who save !
I dare not meet that awful face,
Going unshriven and without grace !
Deep in no grave can I find rest
With this dark secret in my breast.
Oh, priest, assoil me, ere the glass
Suffer those slipping sands to pass.

Pain at my heart a dagger pricks —
Quick, to my lips the crucifix!
Life, like those sands, is slipping fast,
And I shall be unsained at last!

Oh, priest, the pang is past.   And now
Let me make haste to tell you how
The thing was done.   For you must see
The wreck I am I could not be
In those lost years.
                         My arm was strong;
My blood went singing such a song
Of life and joy along my veins,
As in May moons and flowery lanes
Lovers go singing proud and glad,
And what I wanted, that I had!
Oh, had I never at the first
Pursued —   Alas, I was accursed!
Oh, had I never —   For Christ's sake,
Were it a dream and I could wake!
But I was young, and what so bold?
Now I am old, old, very old!
Now I am nothing but a pain —
Oh, priest, the agony again!
Sign me the sign of the cross!   Draw near!
Wait, I will breathe it in your ear.
'T was I — Nay, start not!   Oh, 't was I
That —   Listen!   Do not let me die
Till I have told you!   Turn your head —
Those eyes, those awful eyes of the dead
Shining like corpse-lights!   Give me breath —
Unsained — unshriven — God!   Is this death!

BRONTË

THERE are two ghosts upon the stair !
One is so slender and so fair —
The grave-light faints upon her hair,
And falls and follows as she stirs
With the old grace that once was hers,
Stirs on that chill and sinuous breath
Blown from the frozen halls of death.
A dream, a film, along the air —
There are two ghosts upon the stair.

There are two ghosts without the door, —
One lofty as when first she wore
The purple of her youth, and bore
Her state like some young queen.   Full white
And icy as the northern light
The death-mask on her face.   And see,
A cold flame where her heart should be !
Calm, bitter calm, and fair and frore,
There are two ghosts without the door.

There are two ghosts beyond the pane —
In all the void and vast inane,
In all the vernal fall of rain,
In all the drifting of the mist,
When winds are high, when winds are whist,
In all the long sighs of the gale,
Two hovering wavering shapes and pale,
In all the wide night's dark domain,
There are two ghosts beyond the pane.

39

IN TITIAN'S GARDEN

On wintry driving of the sleet,
Between those graves whose furrows meet,
She sees a yearning face and sweet.
All night she hears the great winds blow,
And sees the wild, white, whirling snow
Sweep up the black vault of the sky,
And sees a shadow fleeting by
That treads the storm with royal feet, —
There are two ghosts upon the sleet.

Out on the high brow of the moor,
Night lifting all her clear-obscure,
Or morn with primal tides washed pure,
While skies and larks together soar,
And the rime glimmers fresh and hoar,
Out in the glorious golden weather,
Knee-deep and lost in plumy heather,
In lonely space from lure to lure
There are two ghosts upon the moor.

And when along heaven's shining coasts
The summer evening leads his hosts
In the great train the pole-star boasts,
She sees from purple hollows shine
Eyes with a sorrow half divine,
And in a mist of stars will note
Ethereal weft of garments float, —
Pressing from faintest farthest posts
In heaven itself there are two ghosts.

BRONTË

Or dreaming there beside the hearth
Of lightsome days of ancient mirth
That cast a bloom upon the earth,
Of shapes that filled those happy years
Seen through the halo of her tears,
She feels them stealing nigh and nigher
To take the last flash of the fire, —
Woe to that house of gloom and dearth,
There are two ghosts beside the hearth!

Sometimes at night about her bed
The moonlight, in a glamour shed,
Puts on the likeness of the dead.
The glamour creeps along the wall,
Far off soft voices seem to fall,
Soft footsteps falter through the room,
She cries, and reaches in the gloom,
And life, and light, and joy are fled, —
There are two ghosts about her bed.

The gentle cunning fails her hand,
Here where they woke, they wrought, they planned,
While day slides o'er the lonesome land,
The needle poised, the pencil prone, —
Pale fingers moving with her own, —
The book, that once strange witchery threw,
Forgotten slipt, — they read it, too, —
Awake, asleep, astir, at stand,
There are two ghosts at her right hand.

What memories nestling in her heart
With wild, sweet wings of longing start!
The things they touched — with awful art —
The clock's dull tick, the walls, the doors, `
The very shadows on the floors,
The old smiles, wake an aching fret.
Barbed with the poison of regret
Each moment gives a keener smart, —
There are two ghosts within her heart!

There are two ghosts upon the stair.
Long since Fame spread his splendid snare;
Love came and camped about her there.
Oh, love was sweet, and life was dear, —
But, hark! those voices, strong and clear,
They wail, they call, she must not stay —
Out, to the open, and away!
Oh, love past death and death's despair,
There are three ghosts upon the stair!

LAMENT

HOW meagre seems the life so briefly doled!
That I who noted in your earliest hour
The dimple in the lovely cheek unfold
With the first smile of all, — that I who told
The promise of your beauty, as some flower
Flaming across the dark days of the year
Promises summer, — that I who in your first
Dear warble had divined the glorious burst

`

LAMENT

Of music in your throat that yet might be
The marvel of some later minstrelsy, —
How meagre seems the life so briefly doled!
That I shall never see that beauty grow
To its meridian, full orbed as the moon
Which great and golden in the mist swims low
And hangs wide-winged in heaven when perfect
    June
Transfigures night, — that I shall never hear
The voice in all the passion of its tune
Sweet, sweet and rich with the unfallen tear,
The stress of love, the whole of life! Ah, me,
I shall be lying in my dust, all mute,
For song the owlet over me shall hoot,
I shall be gone, like the loose leaf from the tree,
The idle leaf that flutters in the blast,
And falls, and sodden with showers returns at last
To the enriching earth.   Nor late, nor soon,
Dead in the dark, shall it be known to me
That you, the one consummate flower and fruit,
Still show all men how goodly is the root!

Thus murmured I when the child's loveliness
With gracious prophecy of lip and brow
Filled all my yearning heart with sweet distress
And longing for the impossible.   And now
Less even than the loose and idle leaf,
A mere blown petal from the blowing bough,
The child is gone, and I grow gray and old.
And still I murmur to my angry grief,
How meagre is the life so briefly doled!

43

THE HOUR OF PEACE

UPON the door-stone sat the wife,
  The twilight falling,
And far below the whippoorwills
  Were softly calling.
The sweet winds dropped upon their way
  Their honeyed plunder,
And slow and clear the night built up
  Its house of wonder.

Within, the child dreamed deep, and saw
  Four angels keeping
Their gentle ward with leaning wings
  About his sleeping.
While singing from the steep below,
  Where shadows slumbered,
Her true love climbed, and in his heart
  His treasures numbered.

And sighing faintly to herself
  With purest pleasure,
Life brimming at her lips to full
  O'erflowing measure,
She marvelled if the happy earth,
  This summer even,
Were not the paved work laid before
  The courts of heaven.

And yet, a cold wind from the cloud
  To snatch in blowing
The little breath between the lips
  So lightly flowing;

44

MOTHER SONG

A pebble underfoot where sheer
    The rock descended —
Ah, Fate! What slender chances held
    Her heaven suspended!

MOTHER SONG

SOFT sleeps the earth in moonlight blest;
Soft sleeps the bough above the nest;
O'er lonely depths the whippoorwill
Breathes one faint note and all is still.
Sleep, little darling; night is long —
Sleep while I sing thy cradle song.

About thy dream the drooping flower
Blows her sweet breath from hour to hour,
And white the great moon spreads her wings,
While low, while far, the dear earth swings.
Sleep, little darling; all night long
The winds shall sing thy slumber song.

Powers of the earth and of the air
Shall have thee in their mother-care,
And hosts of heaven, together prest,
Bend over thee, their last, their best.
Hush, little darling; from the deep
Some mighty wing shall fan thy sleep.

ON AN OLD WOMAN SINGING

SWEET are the songs that I have heard
From green boughs and the building bird ;
From children bubbling o'er with tune
While sleep still held me half in swoon,
And surly bees hummed everywhere
Their drowsy bass along the air ;
From hunters and the hunting-horn
Before the day-star woke the morn ;
From boatmen in ambrosial dusk,
Where, richer than a puff of musk,
The blossom breath they drifted through
Fell out of branches drenched with dew.

And sweet the strains that come to me
When in great memories I see
All that full-throated quiring throng
Go streaming on the winds of song ; —
Her who afar in upper sky
Sounded the wild Brunhilde's cry,
With golden clash of shield and spear,
Singing for only gods to hear ;
And her who on the trumpet's blare
Sang Angels Ever Bright and Fair,
Her voice, her presence, where she stood,
Already part of angelhood.

But never have I heard in song
Sweetness and sorrow so prolong
Their life — as muted music rings
Along vibrating silver strings —

THE STERN CHASE

As when, with all her eighty years,
With all her fires long quenched in tears,
A little woman, with a look
Like some flower folded in a book,
Lifted a thin and piping tone,
And like the sparrow made her moan,
Forgetful that another heard,
And sang till all her soul was stirred.

And listening, oh, what joy and grief
Trembled there like a trembling leaf!
The strain where first-love thrilled the bars
Beneath the priesthood of the stars;
The murmur of soft lullabies
Above dear unconsenting eyes;
The hymns where once her pure soul trod
The heights above the hills of God —
All on the quavering note awoke,
And in a silent passion broke,
And made that tender tune and word
The sweetest song I ever heard.

THE STERN CHASE

OH, call to that bright ship To-morrow!
Hail, hail her: Ahoy! Ship Ahoy!
Oh, tell us the secret of sorrow,
    And what is the measure of joy!

Oh, hear you no faint cry returning
    The cry that we trumpet her thus?
The sun on her sky-sail is burning,
    Oh, is there no signal for us?

The mists make a moment's erasure,
    Tossing and silver and slow;
Diaphanous, tremulous, azure,
    They fold her in shadows of snow.

A moment the winds fall upon her;
    As a cloud does, she bursts into bloom;
The great waves fawn, doing her honor;
    She glimmers away into gloom.

And the secret of sorrow we never
    Shall hear with the far cry : Ahoy!
Forever, forever, forever
    Escapes us the measure of joy!

PARADISE

THE light lay on the gates, the light
    Sent from no moon nor any star,
And in the radiance strange blooms wild and white,
    White as the mists of morning are
Smitten by sun and storm and shower,
Climbed, ever climbed, a living tower,
Where the life shook in spray and spire,
    With hidden depths half orbed in dew,
    With garlands, an innumerous crew,

PARADISE

Swinging in splendid leaf and brier,
And the high heaven stooped in sad desire,
And far the fragrance streamed, and far the fire.

But heavily the midnight gloomed
   Beyond, o'er all things dear and sweet,
Where the hushed cedars in the lustre loomed
   And cast the darkness at their feet, —
Loomed in the surge of hoary flame
The archangel, burning in vast shame,
Shed on the broad and blenching skies,
   Shed moveless from his sword whose guard
   The way with white transplendence barred, —
Or from insufferable eyes, —
For, in the shadow where all shadow dies,
Black, black behind the gates lay Paradise.

And as they went, they two alone,
   They two, away from Paradise,
One smiled upon them from a happier zone,
   Vaporous, and blushing, and from eyes
Violets with Hesper in their dew,
And murmured, "Though the gates for you
No more unclose, oh, wherefore go
   So far? For underneath these walls
   Once, only once, when Young Love calls,
With music winding wide and low,
They who come after you shall surely know
How sweet the winds of Paradise do blow."

4

Then as their steps stayed at the sigh
  Of low boughs drooping in a wood,
With wings that touched the earth and touched the
    sky
They knew a still dim angel stood.
"Grace do I bear. In Eden's stead
Enter the Eden here," he said.
"Where unforgotten odors creep,
  The rivers out of Eden fall,
  The rose-leaves drift across the wall,
And breathed from ivory flutes shall sweep
Soft measures round you lying dark and deep
Folded within the Paradise of Sleep!"

AT THE POTTER'S

THERE were two vases in the sun.
    A bit of common earthenware,
A rude and shapeless jar, was one.
  The other — could a thing more fair
Be made of clay ? Blushed not so soft
  The almond blossom in the light ;
  A lily's stem was not so slight
With lovely lines that lift aloft
    Pure grace and perfectness full-blown ;
And not beneath the finger tip
So smooth, or pressed upon the lip,
  The velvet petal of a rose.
  Less fair were some great flower that blows
    In a king's garden, changed to stone!

50

AT THE POTTER'S

King's gardens do not grow such flowers —
    In a dream garden was it blown !
Fine fancies, in long sunny hours,
    Brought it to beauty all its own.
With silent song its shape was wrought
    From dart of wing, from droop of spray,
    From colors of the breaking day,
Transfigured in a poet's thought.
      At last, the finished flower of art —
The dream-flower on its slender stem —
What fierce flames fused it to a gem !
    A thousand times its weight in gold
    A prince paid, ere its price was told,
      Then set it on a shelf apart.

But through the market's gentle gloom,
    Crying his ever-fragrant oil,
That should anoint the bride in bloom,
    That should the passing soul assoil,
Later the man with attar came,
    And tossed a penny down and poured
    In the rude jar his precious hoard.
What perfume, like a subtile flame,
      Sprang through its substance happy starred !
Whole roses into blossom leapt,
Whole gardens in its warm heart slept !
    Long afterward, thrown down in haste,
    The jar lay, shattered and made waste,
      But sweet to its remotest shard !

THE KING'S DUST

" THOU shalt die," the priest said to the king.
    "Thou shalt vanish like the leaves of spring.
Like the dust of any common thing
   One day thou upon the winds shalt blow ! "
" Nay, not so," the king said. " I shall stay
While the great sun in the sky makes day ;
Heaven and earth, when I do, pass away.
   In my tomb I wait till all things go ! "

Then the king died. And with myrrh and nard,
Washed with palm-wine, swathed in linen hard,
Rolled in naphtha-gum, and under guard
   Of his steadfast tomb, they laid the king.
Century fled to century; still he lay
Whole as when they hid him first away, —
Sooth, the priest had nothing more to say,
   He, it seemed, the king, knew everything.

One day armies, with the tramp of doom
Overthrew the huge blocks of the tomb ;
Swarming sunbeams searched its chambered gloom,
   Bedouins camped about the sand-blown spot.
Little Arabs, answering to their name,
With a broken mummy fed the flame,
Then a wind among the ashes came,
   Blew them lightly, — and the king was not !

52

A WINTER'S NIGHT

CAPTIVE

WHEN in the dark of some despairing dream
    Sorrow has all her will with me, and ease
Is full forgotten, through her dear degrees
Steals Music, beckoning with a hand supreme
For me to follow.   Straight I see the gleam
    Where the winds dip them in the far bright seas
    That roll and break about the Hebrides,
See white wings flash and hear the sea-birds scream.

Or it may be in palace gardens falls
    The moonlight on wide roses, where the swell
Of one great lover's heart in passion calls
    To deeps in other hearts.   And, listening, well
I know, while sink my slow dissolving walls,
    So Music lured Eurydice from hell.

A WINTER'S NIGHT

COME, close the curtains, and make fast the
    door,
    Pile high the logs, and let the happy room
    Red as the rose on wall and ceiling bloom,
And bring your golden flagons forth and pour
Full drinking of some ancient summer's store
    Of spice and sweetness, while to ruddy gloom
    The fire falls.   And lest one hear sound of
        doom
Let music sing old ditties o'er and o'er.

Yet shall you never make the door so fast
  That no moan echo on the song, no shape
  Dull the wine's fragrance and the blaze obscure
And breathe the dark chill of the outer blast,
  Till you shall turn and shudder to escape
  The awful phantom of the hungry poor !

CRUSADERS

WITH leaping steeds and shrilling trumpet-
    blast,
  Glitter of spears and wind-blown banners blest,
  A cloud of dreams of deathless deed and hest
In domes and deserts where the East was vast,
Rode the Crusaders. Far they rode and fast
  From heathen hands the Sepulchre to wrest ;
  And kingdoms shook before their mighty quest,
The bounds of empire changed as they swept past.

To-day, where sound of sorrow has enticed,
  Fearless, afoot, through mire of field and fen,
Armed only with the mail of love unpriced,
  Where hosts flame wide or darkness makes its
    den,
The glad knights seek the Sepulchre of Christ
Within the bodies and the souls of men !

54

IN THE TIME OF THE AFTERMATH

IN THE TIME OF THE AFTERMATH

THOUGH flame and spice and flower
   Are fallen and dead,
Yet mantling all the sphere
   Of fragrance fled
Some unknown country's airs
   Strange sweetness shed,
And fulness of content
   Broods overhead.

For far afield the soul
   In quiet goes
Where wrapt in azure bloom
   The distance glows,
Where redder droops the leaf
   Than any rose,
And softer than the west
   The south wind blows.

Down dim depths drops the moon
   His golden barque —
And if the mist comes chill
   The night comes dark,
The great sky has no star,
   The hill no spark,
Yet from the outer vast
   What music, hark!

IN TITIAN'S GARDEN

THE TRYST

OUT of the darks and deeps of space,
　Where worlds in awful shadow swim,
I came to meet the ancient sun,
　Obeying all my bond with him.

Wrapped in the glimmer of my scarf,
　My wefts of silver brede and lace,
Woven of stars and winds, I pressed,
　And felt his glory on my face.

When, lo, along my hurrying way
　A shining fillet he had lost,
Or, sooth, another sphere, a star
　That into being he had tost.

A ball of swirling fire, fierce waves
　Of molten jewels leaping fast
And shattering crests of flame and jets
　Of kindling spume, I saw and passed.

Æons of ages, and again
　On my parabolas I swept
Where, lapped in opalescent films,
　The fire-ball rolled and, dreaming, slept.

And yet new ages, and I saw
　In green of vasty forest shade
That sphere enfolded, and in seas
　Where nameless monsters plunged and played.

56

THE TRYST

Once more from darks and deeps of space
　To meet my mighty love I sprung :
Lo, the blue sky, the fleecy cloud ;
　Mooned with soft light the planet swung.

And there were temples on the heights,
　And homes beneath the fruited trees,
And never had I seen before
　Beings so beautiful as these.

They blushed, they smiled, they laughed, they
　　loved ; —
　Fain would I pause before I pass.
What songs they sang !　But then what tears
　They wept !　And there were graves, alas !

Born of that whorl of fire-mist, now
　A little less than gods, they sought
In vain the secret of the stars,
　The mystery of their own thought.

Away, away !　Tremendous whiles
　Shall lapse ; but one day, seamed and charred,
I find this soft and gleaming world
　A shrunken ball, a lifeless shard.

And when at last, perchance, I come,
　The elemental force withdrawn,
Of light, of heat, of motion, life,
　In that place Nothingness shall yawn.

Away! My master and my lord,
  Still drawn by thy almighty will,
Though worlds be born in purple depths,
  Though worlds shall fail, I seek thee still.

What shudder sways me? ah, what chill
  Shakes all my splendor as I flee?
Can loss like that be ours? Oh, love,
  Can that fate fall on such as we?

THE STORY OF THE ICEBERG

HOW weary the ice-river grew
  In those dark months of winter night,
And, poised upon his lofty cliff,
  Longed, longed, for other worlds and flight.

What use was all his mighty mould,
  With none to wonder and admire
The light and color that he held,
  The moonstone gleam, the opal fire!

In vain the mother glacier showed
  Pale altars answering with cold rites
The flashes of eternal stars,
  The lances of the northern lights;

A band of sunbeams came that way,
  Tempted, and touched, and lured him on, —
Wild dreams of suns and southern skies, —
  A wrench, a plunge, and he was gone.

58

THE STORY OF THE ICEBERG

With swift embrace the billows swelled
  To meet him, leaping twice and thrice
In thunder, ere they led him forth,
  King of a world of floating ice.

Down, down, by viewless currents drawn,
  His huge mass underneath the sea,
His lofty tops enskyed, he moved
  Like some vast fleet in majesty, —

Out from the dark, mysterious North,
  With all its glamour, every night
Tingling with unforgotten dreams,
  And every day flood-full of light.

The white bear slumbered in his caves;
  The sunbeams played about his tips ;
Down, down he bore to summer seas
  And crashed his way through sinking ships.

And drowning sailors saw on high
  Those icy walls where surges tossed,
Descended out of heaven, a pile
  Of jewelled splendor fired in frost.

Lapis and turquois pierced with light
  To sapphire, emerald hollows paled
To beryl, topaz burning clear
  In flames of chrysolite, he sailed.

IN TITIAN'S GARDEN

Down, down to equatorial seas
    Still slowly drifting, — ah, how sweet
These soft caresses of the tide
    Far in the depths about his feet !

How tenderly this morning gleam
    Saluted all his shining spires,
That far away the voyager saw
    Tipped with the blaze of ruby fires !

How ardently through warm south winds
    The stresses of the noontide beat,
Till brooks burst forth far up his sides,
    Dissolving in a fervent heat.

Now plumed with streaming smoke he went,
    Now but a cloud of amethyst,
The ghost of glory, weird and white,
    Now wrapt within a world of mist.

The sweet and treacherous currents still
    Around his weakening bases whirled,
The great throat of the hurricane
    Tremendous blasts against him hurled.

Into blue air he crept ; and now
    Those sunbeams armed with javelins swarmed,
A hostile legion, fierce and fain,
    And all his awful beauty stormed.
60

THE MAKING OF THE PEARL

Ah, for that dim, dark home once more,
    Those lances of the northern lights!
Then his tops bent them to their fall,
    The wide seas rose and drowned his heights.

And, but a hulk of crumbling ice,
    Within the deep he found his grave,
Stranded upon a hidden key,
    And washed to nothing by a wave.

THE MAKING OF THE PEARL

SO soft, so warm, the water lay,
    Its chambers paved with amberous lights,
The sunbeams sliding there forgot
    Their home among the skyey heights.

With the rose-tangle's stems they played,
    They blushed beneath the purple dulse,
They swung from tide to tide, and gave
    All swimming things their joyous pulse.

The little creature at their touch
    Felt the fresh force of gathering cells,
And happy seemed this rhythmic life
    That swept its currents through his shells.

Happy the swell of bay and bight
    Dimpling with kisses of a wind
Blown from the royal cinnamon,
    From jasmine and from tamarind.

IN TITIAN'S GARDEN

Happy the shadow of the palms
   Seemed to him, wavering o'er his reef,
Happy the rippling scarf of light
   Tossed from the long banana leaf.

Firmer he fixed him to his rock,
   And wider opened to the tide
That softly rose, and fell, and left
   A grain of sand along his side.

A tiny rasping grain of sand
   It was, whose never-ceasing prick
Dispelled the charm of summer seas
   And pierced him to the very quick.

Ah, what a world of trouble now!
   But straight he bent him to the strife,
And poured around that hostile thing
   The precious ichor of his life.

And storms could stoop and stir the deeps
   To blackness, but he heeded not, —
The universe had nothing now
   For him but that one fatal spot.

The color of the foam, the light
   Of heaven across translucent seas,
Flicker of wings and silver scales, —
   He wrapped the pain with things like these.

62

THE MAKING OF THE PEARL

A trail of jewels in the gleam
　　The dolphins dart, above, below,
With sinuous side and silvery flash,
　　Roll a great eye on him and go.

He saw them only as he felt
　　Sore scathe beneath his mantle lay,
And mending as he could his hurt
　　He spent himself day after day.

Or halcyons rocking on the wave,
　　Or sailing birds of Paradise,
Softly their plumes swept upper air,
　　Idly his ooze received their dyes.

And summer moons might draw the floods
　　With their white magic and wide calm
Shed from the wells of midnight blue, —
　　He knew but never felt their balm.

And as some singer's bitterest woe
　　Has fed the song we love to hear,
So all the trouble of his life
　　Was glorified in this one tear.

What mattered then the swarthy shape
　　That cleft the wave with plunge and whirl
And snatched him into death and doom ?
　　His life was lived in that great pearl.

IN TITIAN'S GARDEN

On some queen's breast it heaves, it falls,
    Changing with every breath its hue,
Sunshine and sea and moon are there,
    The sorrow of a lifetime, too !

THE UNDER LIFE

CLEAR were the waters of the Gulf
    As some great crystal's lucent play,
Clear as the tides of lustrous air
    That wash about the breaking day.

And leaning o'er the boat she saw,
    Where the dull green sea-apron grows,
Wattling of sunbeams, netted flames
    Of liquid blue, of tender rose.

The purple mussel there she saw,
    And saw the coral-tree uplift
Stems of white blossom-stars across
    The shells of many a rainbowed drift.

She saw the sea-anemones
    Parting their petals in each cleft,
And on the spangled floor the wreck
    The pearly nautilus had left.

And fairy fountains in the sea,
    She saw the live sponge playing there,
And passing, sighed for very joy
    Of life and beauty everywhere.

64

THE UNDER LIFE

Long since into those pleasant depths
   Swam lightly forth the new-born sponge,
Glad of his life far underneath
   The long wave's melancholy plunge.

The suckling of the generous flood,
   Freely he went, till when the ledge
Splintered and shelved he made him fast
   Where many currents swept the edge.

Their heavy folds his kindred swayed
   Dreamily round his dwelling-place,
Lifted their golden cups, and wove
   Their fragile fans of rosy lace.

And drawing in and out the streams
   Of the life-laden sea, he fed,
His silken fibres spun, and all
   His tissues filled and overspread.

Doubtless he felt fate's perfect flower
   Bloomed there in his dim growth and dense :
No phantom came to give him dream
   Of more through any unborn sense.

Yet, in the gloom of chasing clouds,
   Through all his labyrinthine ways,
He yearned toward light, unsunned by gleam
   Of lovelier life, of wider ways.

5   65

What wider ways for him, indeed,
　　Till æons swept his type along?
Blind, blind to lovelier life, and deaf
　　To whisper of an ordered song.

His powers, the shadow of his needs,
　　Answered no touch of outer storms,
No sound of slipping keels above,
　　No light of over-leaning forms.

And nothing sketched on his dark wont
　　Hint of the rower's rhythmic grace,
Hint of the child that o'er him shed
　　The lovely shining of her face, —

She, fairer than the dawn in bloom,
　　The blue of heaven within her eye,
Her hair like sunshine, and delight
　　Of conscious being in her sigh.

The ripple swelled, light fell the oar,
　　Her hand trailed where the bubbles swim;
She passed — the dull sponge never knew
　　That such a being smiled on him!

THE STORY OF THE FLOWER

A SPOTLESS thing enough, they said,
　　The drift, perchance, from foreign lands,
Washed in atop of mighty tides
　　And lightly left along the sands.

THE STORY OF THE FLOWER

Was it the treasure of some shell ?
  Some islander's forgotten bead ?
A wave-worn polyp from the reef ?
  The gardener said, " It is a seed."

" Bury it," said he, " in the soil.
  The earth will quicken here, as there,
With vital force ; — so fair the seed,
  The blossom must be wondrous fair ! "

Ah, woe, to lose the ample breath
  Of the salt wastes !   To see no more
The sacrifice of morning burn
  And blot the stars from shore to shore.

Ah, woe, to go into the dark !
  Was it for this, the buoyant slide
Up the steep surge, the flight of foam,
  The great propulsion of the tide ?

To lose the half-developed dream
  Of unknown powers, the bursting throe
Of destinies to be fulfilled,
  And go into the dark — ah, woe !

But the mould closed above the seed
  Relentlessly ; and still as well
All life went on ; the warm winds blew ;
  The strong suns shone ; the soft rains fell.

IN TITIAN'S GARDEN

Whether he slept, or waited there
  Unconscious, after that wild pang, —
Who knows? There came to him at last
  A sense as if some sweet voice sang;

As if, throughout the universe,
  Each atom were obeying law
In tuneful order. In his heart
  He felt the same deep music draw.

And one sharp thrill of tingling warmth
  Divided him ; as if the earth
Throbbed through him all her stellar might
  With the swift pulse of some new birth.

Up the long spirals of his stems
  What currents coming from afar,
What blessedness of being broke, —
  Was he a blossom or a star ?

Wings like their own the great moths thought
  His pinions rippling on the breeze, —
Did ever a king's banner stream
  With such resplendent stains as these ?

Over what honey and what dew
  His fragrant gossamers uncurled !
Forgotten be that seed's poor day,
  Free, and a part of this high world !
68

THE HOLY LAND

A world of winds, and showers aslant,
    With gauzy rainbows everywhere,
Cradled in silken sunshine, rocked
    In skies full of delicious air !

Ah, happy world, where all things live
    Creatures of one great law, indeed ;
Bound by strong roots, the splendid flower, —
    Swept by great seas, the drifting seed !

THE HOLY LAND

ARE they still there — those solemn shapes,
    Those mountains swimming in the light,
The rainbow pulsing in the cloud,
    The torrent tumbling from the height ?

Ah, many a twilight when I heard
    My mother lingeringly repeat
Their legends, in my childish mind
    I put the shoes from off my feet.

Over the plain of Mamre then
    In lovely awe I softly went,
At night I spelled the stars, at noon
    Sat in the doorway of the tent.

Through cloven pass, down flying lines,
    In fire and cloud, in storm and stress,
I wandered with the tribes across
    The desert of the wilderness.

69

IN TITIAN'S GARDEN

I saw the tabernacle then
    Its blue and scarlet curtains blow ;
And came in Zif, the blossom month,
    Upon the palms of Jericho.

I trembled at the answering call
    From Ebal and from Gerizim ;
Far in the temple stood beneath
    Vast silent golden cherubim.

The high-priest's bells and pomegranates
    Made me a sweet and happy din,
And from the porch I heard the blast
    Of trumpets blow the new moon in.

How fair the mountains where the maids
    Went mourning four days in the year,
While haply from the farther slopes
    White bulls of Bashan bellowed clear !

Sweet the high pastures where one cried,
    While the great stars fell back in flame,
'Lift up your heads, ye gates !' and song
    Through the blue blaze of morning came.

The fire fell low ; I felt the thrill
    Of viewless messengers, the room
Grew dark, and Hermon's dome of snow
    Broke forth and glistened in the gloom.

THE HOLY LAND

Gathered the dews, the trickling brooks
    Ran down, and swollen with many streams,
By purpling peaks, by valley fords,
    The Jordan rolled across my dreams.

He came, the Shepherd of the Sheep,
    Who knew all sorrow that there is,
And up and down the land I went,
    My little hand fast held in his.

And sometimes from Bethesda's pool
    A slow still angel stepped to me,
And sometimes all the air returned
    The perfume poured at Bethany.

And out of shores of far delight,
    Bringing great dream, great memory,
I saw the stars come trembling down
    Into the Sea of Galilee.

Gray were the leaves of Olivet,
    And wet Gethsemane's dark sod,
And love and tears went all his way,
    Or were he man or were he God!

And still for me, in other light,
    In finer air, by morn or even,
A place of dream, the Holy Land
    Hangs midway between earth and heaven.

THE LEPERS

HAS fortune found you out too late,
With none to enter on your state ?
Has love saluted you while death
Hovers to snatch the failing breath ?
Or joy come only when the will
To welcome him is numbed and still,
And all the senses at their close
Are withered as last summer's rose ?

———

There were four lepers at the Gate,
All day they sat and cursed their fate.
For them there were no woman's smiles,
No children's lips and joyous wiles ;
No blush of maiden, and no hand
To soothe the ail, flower-soft and bland ;
An aching blotch upon the scene,
They veiled their lips and cried, " Unclean ! "

Beneath the walls in sullen pride
The hostile camp stretched far and wide,
The pomp and power of Syria's crown
Beleaguering the royal town,
Till in the dark streets, day by day,
The King met Famine, gaunt and gray ; —
Mothers were mad and sucklings died —
" Hunger is king, not I ! " he cried.

" Come ! " said the lepers. " Let us go
And try the mercy of the foe.

72

THE LEPERS

There is no food within the town —
We can but die if we go down —
And here we surely die.'' And slow
Down to the camp the lepers go,
Perchance a crust to find, perchance
Wine that should make their thick blood dance.

The twilight ebbed to purple dark —
How still the great plain lay, and hark!
These captains, used to war's alarms,
How sound they sleep upon their arms!
Nor asses bray, nor stallions stamp,
There is no breath in all the camp ;
Struck with tumultuous fright, the host
Has vanished like a morning ghost !

But as the headlong press took wings,
Smote by the fear of Desert Kings
Helping Samaria, where they flung
The golden vessels there they rung
Still vibrant ; silver armor shone
Like moonbeams on the stream ; a throne
Wanted this purple ; and these gems
Were snatched from princes' diadems.

The lepers halt them there alone —
The gleaming treasure is their own !
They hug the jewelled vase ; they seize
The splendid raiment as they please.

73

Till suddenly, with burning eyes,
Each stares in terrible surprise —
Stained, stained with their eternal soil,
They are four lepers in the spoil !

SONG AND THE PROPHET'S SOUL

THEN cried the King of Judah to the others —
The three swart kings shaken with shuddering
fear —
" What is the Lord's will with our way, O
Brothers !
Is there no prophet here ? "
" Alas ! " the youth a-fire with power, a-shiver
With outland gems, had wailed, " The Lord
this three
Hath called together that he might deliver
Them to their enemy ! "
For fast on the bright edge of bitter battle,
Out of red Edom, Edom the accurst,
In the dry torrent-beds the hosts, the cattle,
Were perishing of thirst.

———

A blaze of wrath and doom, the waiting prophet
Towered o'er the rock-rent valley. " Ask,"
he cried,
" The seers of the Sidonian woman of it,
Who at the Kishon died ! "
For like great seas beneath the horned moon dark-
ening,

74

SONG AND THE PROPHET'S SOUL

The man of God felt all his spirit swell,
The son of the Phœnician princess hearkening —
That fierce Queen Yzabel!
" As the Lord liveth, but for Judah pressing,
Maker of gods, I would not look toward thee!
Yet for his sake — if sooth there be a blessing —
The minstrel bring to me! "

———

The minstrel played.   And with the harp's wide
 ringing
Surely that moment was a marvel wrought,
Seraphic credence in serene flight winging
 The prophet's Heaven-domed thought.

There swept the camel-train, the while he listened,
 Bearing the ancient Priest of the Most High
Where the long lances of the desert glistened
 Coming from victory, —
Without descent, and having no beginning
 Nor end of life, who brought the bread and
 wine
To the young chief fresh from his battle-winning,
 In sacramental sign.

There crossed the angels, climbing and descending
 The shining ladder leaning on a flame; —
There one in darkness with the Lord pretending
 Wrestled and overcame.

There under crystal wall and crested hollow
  Swings out the sea-way sundered bare and broad,
And he who leads where all the pale press follow
  In Horeb spoke with God.
Plunge on, plunge on, ye golden wheels, ye horses!
  Pharaoh and princes, drown in the deep sea!
The green wave curls above your sunken corses,
  My host pass over free!

Then throng the captains, blustering banners blow-
    ing,
  All the great fathers of innumerous lines,
Long breathe the horns, hosannas heavenward
    throwing,
  And the Shekinah shines!
Close to the skies they range; by morn and even
  Companion God! For them the lightnings smite,
For them the suns stand still! They fight from
    Heaven,
  Stars in their courses fight!

Soft flows the tune. And all along the mountains
  With strangely sweet sufficing songs and wild,
The white-scarfed virgins tell the shadowy fountains
  The wrong of Galaad's child.

Soft! for he hears the women drawing water
  And singing at the well, " Spring up, O well!"
The deep, cool well — the mother sings, the
    daughter,
  Through peaceful Israel.

SONG AND THE PROPHET'S SOUL

Soft! for about the flock what clear strains dally
   And soar on skimming mists, where listening far
Over the blue bloom of the midnight valley
   Trembles the wandering star!
Soft, soft! The beautiful boy-shepherd only
   Answer these echoes from the mountain-wall,
Low the unwilling lion far and lonely,
   And the dark soul of Saul.

How full it throbs, with such luxurious warble
   They heard in Tadmor in the Wilderness,
Stretched upon ivory couches, empire's bauble
   Lavished on loveliness!

Sound low, sound hoarse, O melody of sorrow!
   As sheep that have no shepherd, scattered wide,
Homeless my people stray some sad to-morrow
   Far from their country-side.

Swell, then, with Miriam's timbrel, silver-clashing,
   With Ehud's clarion, with Deborah's chant!
Sword of the Lord and Gideon, once more flashing,
   The flying desert daunt!
Swell, hymn of joy! The men of war, the peerless,
   Loom through the cloud — Manoah's son, the
      vast,
And he that hewed the Anakim, and fearless
   Shamgar, that thunderblast!
And the three mighty men who plunged down
   straightway

77

Through the dark foe, when the King said to them,
  " Oh that one gave me water from the gateway
  And well of Bethlehem ! ''
And he, the mightiest, whose arms have broken
  The bow of steel, in whose tremendous clasp
The giant's brand is light, who holds in token
  The kingdoms in his grasp !
Strong rings thy sword, thou fair of eyes and
    splendid !
  Stronger thy voice, and sweeter rings than strong,
Thou where the Spirit of the Lord descended
  When the heavens dropped with song !

Hath any god such men as this great seven,
  These godlike in the strength of their desires ?
Hath Ishtar, with her blossom-moons in Heaven,
  Hath Bel with all his fires ?
Swell, O supreme, O song in thy glad fitness,
  Thy stormy joys, thy heart-dissolving pains !
Long since, the Lord commanded thee a witness
  On Moab's awful plains !
The Lord who came from Sinai, our Defender,
  Who rose from Seir, and out of Paran shined,
In his right hand a fiery law whose splendor
  Dazzled the heathen blind !

Break, break, ye furthest skies ! Lo, flashing, rending,
  The Chariot and the horsemen !   And the hand
Of the Lord laid on me, all song transcending —
  Go ! And possess the land !

TWO ANGELS

Fallen was the music. Still the jubilant story
  Sang on there as the wind sang through the
    strings,
And into spaces flushed with solemn glory
  Gazed the three silent kings —
Gazed and beheld, in conquering alliance,
  Foreshadow of burnt-offering's crimson pall,
Where the beleaguered slew in mad defiance
  His firstborn on the wall,
And gazing saw the clouds drip blood and ashes —
  The awful likeness of a funeral pyre —
The heart of Heaven burst in monstrous flashes —
  A soul go up in fire!

TWO ANGELS

TWO angels out of darkness born,
  All unaware of bloom or scathe,
Hung on the outer edge of morn, —
  And one was Doubt, and one was Faith.

Doubt spread his gray and mighty plume
  Beyond the bounds of space and night,
And round dim depths and gulfs of gloom
  Swept with an ever-circling flight.

But Faith, with eyes that only knew
  Immeasurable light above,
Sprang upward through the quivering blue
  And rested in the heart of Love.

79

IN TITIAN'S GARDEN

BY NIGHT

SHE leaned out into the midnight,
And the summer wind went by,
The scent of the rose on its silken wing
And a song its sigh.

Deep in the tarn the mountain
A mighty phantom gleamed,
Shadow and silver the floating cloud
Over it streamed.

And, in depths below, the waters
Answered some mystic height,
As a star stooped out of the depths above
With its lance of light.

And she thought, in the dark and the fragrance,
How vast was the wonder wrought
If the sweet world were but the beauty born
In its Maker's thought.

And up from the tarn and its phantom
Wandered her weary glance
Where that star, as the awful ranks wheeled by,
Held its shining lance.

And a sudden sweetness of sorrow
From the far lone whip-poor-will
Touched her to tears, while she searched those
depths,
Cavernous — still.

80

A WEED

Was there love in those infinite spaces?
　Was there life for the life dropped here?
Oh, what was the way to the life and love
　Of that unknown sphere!

Then star over star stood marshalled,
　White splendor beyond them broke,
And a door was opened in heaven there
　While she blindly spoke.

And a gladness dearer than dreaming
　Filled the heart that was sad and sore,
And almost she heard a murmuring voice,
　" I am the Door."

A WEED

I AM so small on this great scale
　Of moons and suns and cosmic ways,
I am so poor in all that rears
　The treasure of transcendent days,
I am so stained if any see
　The shrinking soul in heaven's white blaze!

So small, alas, so poor, so stained, —
　What glance that meets the idle soul
Can linger there with least delight,
　Nor spurn it with a beggar's dole?
Can heavenly help to feed it flow,
　Can heavenly love about it roll?

6　　　　　　　　　　　　　　　81

And going sadly on my way
   A little flower looks up at me,
A worthless weed beside the path,
   That has no honey for the bee,
Nor any beauty that the eye,
   The thrall of beauty, waits to see.

Because I am as worthless too,
   I pluck the thing that has no use
Nor loveliness.   Its fainting breath
   Makes for a moment half excuse —
Lo, the precision of its lines
   Star orbits to a leaf reduce !

Over its face the twilight tints
   Are painted, evening skies less fair.
How lightly swept the master-hand
   To make that petal melt in air !
What subtle thought was crowded here,
   How exquisite the procreant care !

The golden eye of day is not
   More golden than its heart set free !
What spent itself on this small flower ?
   What sends its brief felicity ?
What lavish to a worthless weed
   Shall not as lavish be to me !

SCRIPTURE

AGAINST the sky the frolic spray
Tossing a mesh of twinkling lines;
Buds, where at dewy dawn of day
The inner dream of color shines;
Heaven midmost of the forest dells
Painted within the lake's deep cup;
The glamour where the dim sea swells
And lets the moon swim slowly up;
The blowing showers that slip and go,
The azure shadows of the snow,
The mist that drifts by cliffs and scars,
The great processional of stars,
Write me the blazon everywhere,
On blue and interfluent air,
Lustre of leaf and sheen of sod,
That beauty is the thought of God.

The morning murmur of the bees —
The hum of wing and sunshine blent;
The summer wind among the trees
In happy fulness of content;
Music of dying thunders' roll
Down cloudy gulf and cloven shelf;
Echo, sweet Echo, like a soul
Singing, still singing, to herself;
The undefined and air-drawn spells,
At evenfall, of distant bells;
That white flower blown in dark and hush —
Song only, and the hermit thrush;

The winding horn, the subtler tune
Of fluting voices, read the rune,
With wash of wave and thrill of clod,
That beauty is the thought of God.

The pristine innocence that meets
Pure passion with a darkling kiss,
And in his purple mantle fleets
Down islands of immortal bliss ;
The smiles that on the hurt thing fall
As tenderly as dove's wings furl
About their nestling ; and withal
The pity lying like a pearl
Deep in the heart ; the strength that yearns
In mothers, and in heroes burns ;
The love that lives for love — that dies ;
The awful joy of sacrifice ;
Inform the answering consciousness —
As white fire through the starry press
Of heaven runs with silence shod —
That beauty is the thought of God.

CLAIRVOYANCE

DARK the shadows close round my sad spirit,
    Encamped in their terrible power,
Encamped like an army besetting
    Some desolate tower.
There is naught, my soul murmurs, but sorrow, —
    What eager endeavor shall dare

CLAIRVOYANCE

These shadows that raise their fell standard
  To mantle the air,
Blown out by the black breath of boding
  Of death and despair.

Then suddenly into the darkness,
  Like the northern lights' radiance, streams
The tale that I read in my childhood,
  That swept through my dreams,
With cohorts of angels, and squadrons
  Of stars with their spears all one way,
Fading out in a wan and white splendor
  At the gray break of day,
Half guessed in the lustre of noontide,
  Half glimpsed in my play.

For, behold, the great prophet was lying
  Hid away in the dim city's bound,
And the Syrian King sent the Captains
  To compass him round,
With the strong men of war, and their chariots,
  And the host of the horsemen and foot,
The treasure of scarlet, the slave girls
  With shawm and with flute,
The bowmen, the slingers, the lances
  In flashing pursuit.

How fair lay the land as the evening
  Shed there its sighing surcease,
And night-fall and dew-fall had spread there
  The purple of peace.

IN TITIAN'S GARDEN

How sweet the song rose from the housetop,
  The tinkle far off from the fold,
While in dim depths all star-sown the mountain
  Still soared rose and gold.
What hush lay beneath the dark rampart,
  What balm the breeze rolled!

But when sunrise struck up from the deserts
  A ray like the blade of a sword,
Whose crests were these set to salute it,
  Whose tents were this horde,
And wet with the morning whose banners,
  That light winds went ruffling, were they,
Whose javelins, whose shields, still pressed forward,
  Whose cries rent their way
Through the glitter and tumult to vanquish
  One man old and gray!

Then the youth who was staff to the seer
  Fared forth in the fresh early hour,
And his heart burst within him confronting
  The Assyrian power.
But the clear-seeing prophet cried, " Fear not!
  For they that be with us are more
Than they that be with them!" And praying,
  Bade turn him where frore
All the dells and the horns of the mountain
  With dew were yet hoar.

86

THE HEAVENLY CAMP

There the opaline cloud slowly lifting,
   The rock darkly dripping, and there —
Lo, the chariots of fire ! Lo, a mightier
   Encampment lay bare !
Shod with lightning, and clothed with the thunder,
   The horse reared, and poised for vast flight,
Troops of stars on their spear-heads, receding
   In infinite light,
Archangels in phalanx of glory
   Burned silent and white.

The chariots of fire, and the horsemen !
   Shall the lad in his innocence see
The help of the hills, and shall nature
   Deny it to me ?
Oh, shadows that close round my spirit
   In the clefts of the rocks haste and hide !
For me, too, the mountain is trembling
   Where heaven's hosts abide,
Great forces are thrilling and arming, —
   God fights on my side !

THE HEAVENLY CAMP

ACROSS the open window blows
  The languorous breathing of the rose,
The young moon drops its ruddy spark
Behind the wood, and all is dark.
Through dreamy hush the river goes,
The purple opens as it flows,
And larger heavens their depths disclose.

IN TITIAN'S GARDEN

Forth in the night I fare, while slow
The still translucent spaces grow
Out of their midnight bloom, as clear
As one great jewel, sphere o'er sphere,
Till tender splendors shed their glow
Far off and infinite, as though
They veiled some unknown country so.

Fain would my wish the seas explore
That break upon that farther shore
In silent thunders, and immerse
From universe to universe
My being, till at last I pour
My love, my longing out before
The Love that lives forevermore.

The swift dawn comes, a rosy flare,
And shuts me with my hope, my care,
In the dear world of glancing dew,
Of blossom-bough and velvet blue.
Yet yonder hangs diviner air,
And all day long I breathe aware
The country of the Lord is there.

EQUATIONS

YOU so sure the world is full of laughter,
  Not a place in it for any sorrow,
Sunshine with no shadow to come after —
  Wait, O mad one, wait until to-morrow !

88

THE STAR IN THE EAST

You so sure the world is full of weeping,
 Only gloom in all the colors seven,
Every wind across a new grave creeping —
 Think, O sad one, yesterday was heaven !

———

Young and strong I went along the highway,
 Seeking Joy from happy sky to sky ;
I met Sorrow coming down a byway, —
 What had she to do with such as I ?

Sorrow with a slow detaining gesture
 Waited for me on the widening way,
Threw aside her shrouding veil and vesture, —
 Joy had turned to Sorrow's self that day !

———

If some great giver give me life,
 And give me love, and give me double,
Shall I not also at his hand
 Take trouble ?

And if through awful gloom I see
 The lightnings of his great will thrusting,
Shall I not, dying at his hand,
 Die trusting ?

THE STAR IN THE EAST

FROM hoary kingdoms of all ancientness,
 Led by a Star they came, —
A Star that dimmed the lustre of the heavens
 Shaking their fleece of flame !

A splendid caravan, from desert depths
   They flashed their royal way ;
Gold wrought, in all strange charactery and gems
   Their housings caught the ray.

The shining stallions arched their necks and rang
   Their jewelled bridle-reins ;
The stately camels stretched like monoliths
   Their shadows on the plains.

Treasure of perfumes and of precious stones
   Weighed them, and wondrous web
Of scarlet cloths woven at the wane of moon
   And at the great sea's ebb ;

And oils, and gums, the ooze of sacred trees
   In sun-imprisoning flecks,
And in their lamps the fire not once relit
   Since priest Melchizedek's.

There little Melchior, King of Nubia, came
   With gold to signify
Possession of the empire of the earth
   And kingship's prophecy.

And Chaldæa's monarch, the old Balthazar,
   Brought incense, for a sign
That prayer and praise should find divinity
   In manger or in shrine.

THE STAR IN THE EAST

But Jasper, black, and of a mighty make,
 And of rich Tarshish king,
Brought neither gold nor incense, but brought
 myrrh,
 For human suffering.

And with them, and before them, the great Star,
 That up the eastern coasts,
Outstripping comets and white-bearded orbs,
 Came leading heaven's hosts.

While all black art of dark astrology,
 With incantations gray
That signs and zodiacs trembled to regard,
 Showed where the young child lay, —

The young child, who, not yet a fortnight old,
 Among the oxen slept,
Where angels hung upon a drooping wing,
 And all the sweet watch kept.

Chiefs of old heathenry, how long, how far,
 They journeyed on their quest !
What tribute and what treasure did they bring
 To greet the holy guest !

What costly travel and what toilsome march
 Were theirs, too, — that great press
Which followed on the way the Magi led
 . Up from the wilderness !

IN TITIAN'S GARDEN

But we, on whom for twice a thousand years
    The Star in the East has shone, —
What hard road do we tread with tender feet
    To make the truth our own ?

Up from what deserts do we hotly spur
    To consecrate our King ?
To God, in Christ or in Humanity,
    What tribute do we bring ?

We look on the immensity of space,
    And count all creeds a song ;
We let the dungeoned prisoner write in blood
    The story of his wrong.

So we but lose no bubble of the wine,
    In the rose crush no sting,
We care not for the pierced divinity, —
    We crown the senses King !

Brief empery, that with the bubble breaks,
    With the rose falls ! whose slaves
Shall revel then but with the loathly worm
    And the dark fruit of graves !

Dart forth your white and awful light, O Star,
    Wither this King to dross !
Lead us a path like that once trod the feet
    Were nailed upon a cross !

PHILLIPS BROOKS

JAMES RUSSELL LOWELL

DYING, he dreamed he entertained a King.
He opened wide those wondrous eyes that
burned
With heaven's own lightning, all his thought con-
cerned
To greet the royal presence.   Not that thing
Of mortal birth, and for a moment crowned
Within a gemmy bauble's glittering bound,
But One for whom gates sempiternal swing,
But One the lifting of whose deathless wing
Disclosed the Infinite toward which he yearned.

O poet ! you who saw, O spirit strong,
Beyond the walls of sense, as they whose sight
Is interpenetrate with quickening light,
Who caught the meaning of seraphic song
And made it earthly music, born of sound,
Far, and more ancient than the rosy round
Of morning, you indeed saw Sovereign Might
Fill all your dying chamber with delight
And lead you to the realm where you belong !

PHILLIPS BROOKS

PERHAPS we do not know how much of God
Was walking with us.
                         Surely not forlorn
Are men, when such great overflow of heaven
Brings down the light of the eternal morn

Into the earth's deep shadows, where they plod,
The slaves of sorrow.
                              Something of divine
Was in his nature, open to the source
Of love, that master of primeval force,
As, answering freshly their unfailing sign,
To the early and the latter rain the sod
Lies bare, and drinking in by morn and even
The precious dews that lift it into flower
Distilled again in fragrance every hour.

I think if Jesus, whom he loved as Lord,
Were here again, in such guise might He go,
So bind all creeds as with a golden cord,
So with the saint speak, with the sinner so.
And then remembering all the torrent's rush
Of praise and blessing o'er the listening hush,
Remembering the lightning of the glance,
Remembering the lifted countenance
White with the prophet's glory that it wore,
With the Holy Spirit shining through the clay,
Prophet — yea, I say unto you, and more
Than a prophet was with us but yesterday!

THE KNIGHT OF PENTECOST

PRONE as he lay before the dim, high altar,
  No strain of any solemn prayer or psalter
    Disquieted the stillness of the night ;
No long roll of the organ's golden thunder,
No voices, keyed to sweet and joyous wonder,
    Fled like a flight of angels into light.

THE KNIGHT OF PENTECOST

The painted panes of the rose-window sparkled
A moment, as some cold star shone and darkled,
  And awful shadows filled the vaulted space.
Prone on the flint he lay and kept his vigil,
All his soul waiting for the sign and sigil
  That should appoint him to his knightly place.

Nor sound nor silence, light nor dark, he noted.
Up from the under-world the slow moon floated,
  And looked upon the trance that held him
    there ;
With half her snowy glimmer stooped and wrapped
    him :
Naught knew he of the gracious bloom that lapped
    him ;
  He waited flame more glorious, sight more fair.

Far, far, the night swept on through deeps un-
    broken,
While his thought, seeking the supremest token,
  Mounted among unknown infinitudes,
Where still beyond his dreaming or his seeing
The Soul that fills the universe with being
  Above all calm, above all tumult, broods.

As if a star burst, with a clang of warning
The great bell tolled the holy hour of morning :
  No blessed chrism had found him where he lay.
He rose like one long worn with weary marches,
And, passing underneath the heavy arches,
  He came out to the open break of day.

Wide, wide, the wash of the free air was flowing,
And high the soft gray flower of dawn was blow-
ing,
    Fresh, fresh, the dewy wind that sighed and
    ceased !
Into eternal heavens the heaven was lifting,
Light, radiant light, across the world was sifting,
    The fire burned on the altar of the east.

Not in the dark the tongue of flame came leaping
Upon his lips, across his forehead sweeping ;
    Not prostrate in great glooms of temple shade :
But while he gazed, one only with his Master,
In deathless circles swelling vast and vaster,
    The dawn, swift-sworded, flashed his accolade.

Glory of argent space all space ensphering !
Sweeter than sound a voice surpassed his hearing !
    Close on his heart he felt great pulses swim !
He knew not as he stood there, trembling, yearn-
ing,
All heaven about him in that moment burning,
    That spirits came and ministered to him.

Weapons of skyey temper had they wrought him,
Deific armor from afar they brought him,
    And bound it on with touches swift and fine.
There stood the good steed ready for his guiding,
Through the dark places of the sad land riding,
    Light for the watchword, Love the countersign.

THE PRAYER OF IBN GEBIROL

A mighty shape, scarfed with the sun uprisen,
Where tears distilled, where spirits were in prison,
   Where doubt went groping, and where dolor lay,
Where in despairing death the dying languished,
Wherever sin, wherever suffering anguished,
   He in their service took his shining way.

And soaring, an aerial apparition,
Ever before him hung a splendid vision,
   Where, far within the sapphire crystalline,
Unstained by wrong, unspotted by a sorrow,
The sweet earth floated in a gleaming morrow,
   And joy welled through it from the heart divine.

Full of the word that made the sunlit weather,
Full of the strength that holds the stars together,
   White with the whiteness of the Holy Ghost,
By all the forces of the day surrounded,
Then rode he forth, his trump of onset sounded,
   All sacrosanct, a Knight of Pentecost.

THE PRAYER OF IBN GEBIROL

BEN YEHUDAH IBN GEBIROL prayed
this prayer:
Master of many mysteries, him they named
The Keeper of the Kabbalah, and all
The Secret Writing of the Law; who spoke
With the vast djinns confederate about
The ivory throne of Solomon the King

7

Unseen in the prodigious splendor there ;
Who with his finger drew the awful lines,
The spheral ways, down which archangels run
Upon their mighty errands.
                     Such strange things —
White magic were they, or the scathe of the brain
Long cramped in midnight poring over signs
At which the scorpion from his cranny gazed
As at his kindred — did men say of him.
But we, forsooth, we know not.   All we know
Is that the thought, outsoaring such device
As the great heaven outsoars the gossamer,
Was his who in one glory of white light
Transfused the many colors of many creeds
While uttering this ascription, prayer, and praise :

Thou art God, he said, and all the living things
Upon this ball that swings in hoary space,
Or that live otherwhere, thy servants are.
And being God, essence of excellence,
Source of all life, soul of the beautiful, —
O sacred soul of souls and life of life,
O dearer than the dearness of delight, —
Felt in the dewy darks of dawn before
The rose flowers out in heaven ; when north
     winds cry
Where the white wonder of the waning moon
Rides high through lonely midnights ; when the
     storms
Hiss in the sea, and hide in shrouded snows ;
Felt in the starry gulfs through which the thought

Sails in meridian ; felt in the mere joy
Of being alive ; and truly when Death smiles,
And reaches forth a strong and tender hand,
No less felt, — thou art God, — and, being God,
All things are thy adorers.
      In no wise
Thy majesty is lessened should they call
On other names than thine — seeming to adore
Other than thou, in midst of blinding light,
Phrah in his fire, or Om within his dream,
Or any precious phantasm that for them
Holds godhead as the jewel holds the spark —
Since all their aim entirely is to come
Nearer to thee, and only thee, and lose
Sense — ay, and self — within the whelming seas
Where broods thy prime, where brims thy blessed-
   ness.
If their way lead to Isis with her lily
Seeking the way herself through glimmering dark,
'T is thou. And if to She'keenah, 't is thou.
If to the immanent divine in man,
And if to the white Christ upon his cross,
Through all, and over all, and under all,
'T is thou.
   What seek they but thy sweetness ? What
But rest upon thy power, — to feel in them
The rushing of thy life ? Are they not thine ?
With thy clear currents of immortal joy
Drown out in them all that is less than thou,
As morning drowns sky-deep the beacon star
Where with wild lightnings wash the lucid tides,

Leaping and shoaling when the day has laid
His beams upon the waters.
                                    Near or far,
Seek they not God? I said.   And thou art God!

Thus, in the dark hot Spanish night long since,
While the white moth about his candle flew
And fluttered out into the larger light
Where the red moon rose in the gap of the hills,
Ben Yehudah Ibn Gebirol paused a space,
As point by point he glossed the mystery
Within the ten Sephiroth, murmuring
The moving music of this joyous cry.

THE WANDERERS

ALL in the middle night, across the crystal
    hollow of the dark,
  Before the black pines' tempest-torn gigantic
    glooms remembered morn,
Heard I, indeed, strange music toss and beat
    about the winds? And, hark,
  Were there no sweet and piercing cries, was
    there no echo of a horn?

For what a glorious company hung out of heaven
    before me there,
  As, leaning forth, along the height I caught the
    glitter of their flight!
100

THE WANDERERS

From depths of termless mystery what shapes were
    these trooped down the air
    Shooting white fire abroad, and clear their
    splendor streaming on the night?

His casque whose ruby led the field was it then
    Mars that swept and gazed?
    In gleaming gauzes veiled about were these the
    Pleiades looked out?
On corselet, belt, and sword, and shield, Orion's
    breathing diamonds blazed?
    White and majestic, Sirius followed upon the
    mighty rout?

And slowly out of dusky space, one, stately, coming
    from afar,
    The fulness of some golden chord marking the
    measure of his ward,
The whole of heaven upon his face, was it the
    bright and morning star,
    Was it but Lucifer that wore the lustre of the
    living Lord?

Or were they, bound in vaster flight, Magnificent
    Existences,
    For firmaments of unknown sky, that paused a
    moment fleeting by
The dark and dreaming earth that night? I only
    know, beholding these,
    Held not my hand a Mightier Hand, an atom of
    the dust were I!

THE TOURNEY

I

THE bugles sung, the banners threw
  Their rippling shadows to and fro,
Forward the knights and horses dashed,
Thundered the earth, and armor clashed
In mighty tune, as on they flew,
As they flew on to meet the foe.
And one in golden cuisses flashed,
And round his voice the echoes pealed,
And with his visor up one wheeled,
And splendidly his beauty bloomed,
And one had roses wet with dew
About his crest, and like the snow
Blown from some peak within the blue
One scarf was with the morning plumed,
And Youth, and Love, and Hope, and Song,
And Joy, and Faith, a gallant crew,
Swift as the arrow from the bow,
Unfaltering they swept along
And cast themselves upon the foe !
And clear they called and bade him yield
Who in his vast, black silence loomed,
And on his steadfast strength they crashed
Full cry, without a dream of dread,
And swords were broke, and bucklers gashed
And lances splintered on his shield
And spun like sleet, and riders reeled,
And fetlock-deep in blood they plashed,
And Youth went down, and no hand steeled

The heart of Hope, and no hand healed
His mortal hurt, and Love was dead,
And Song was fallen, and Faith had fled, —
And Death was master of the field!

II

THEN Death his helmet laid aside,
And with imperial lustre shined
The countenance but half-divined.
I had no quarrel with their pride, —
They were so beautiful, he sighed.
They would not have me to their friend,
Poor fools, or they had never died!
Poor children of the dark, and blind,
Who could not guess the smile I hide,
Nor borrow of the strength I lend.
Had they struck hands with me, in truth,
Love had immortal been, and Youth.
And Faith should still the stars ascend
To farther stars.   And tenting there
The skies had bent round Joy.   Alas,
With their own brand they laid them low!
Now they are ashes, let them go
On that light wind shall chance to pass
Where they lie trodden in the grass.
They were a feeble folk, forsooth!
Forget they ever were so fair,
Forget they breathed the lightsome air,
And let my wailing trumpets blow
It was not Death that was their foe!

O MUSIC

LAST night I heard a harper strike his strings
    all suddenly and sweetly,
And one sang with him in a voice blown like a
    flute upon the dark,
And as a bird's wings climb the air, forever palpi-
    tating fleetly,
The song soared, and I followed it, lost where the
    panting echoes hark.
The song soared like a living soul in naked beauty
    white and stark,
Commanding all the powers of tune with solemn
    spells of subtle might,
A flute, a bird, a living soul, the song swept by
    me in the night !

Commanding all the powers of tune, commanding
    all the powers of being,
While on the borderland of sleep half lapped in
    dreams my senses stirred,
Heaven after heaven the strain laid bare, sweet
    secret after secret freeing,
And all the deeps of music broke about my spirit
    as I heard.
And past and present were as naught within that
    trance of rapture blurred,
And heights where white light seethed, and depths
    night-blue and full of singing stars,
Were mine to tread the while that tune beat out
    the passion of its bars !

Then I remembered me of Saul, the young man mighty and victorious,
While towering dark and beautiful anointed on the roadside king,
And over him a fuller chrism streamed sempiternally and glorious,
The dew of dawn, the flush of day, that morning of an ancient spring.
And faring silent on his way, he lifted not his voice to sing,
He saw no glow upon the hills, upon the sky he saw no bloom,
Earth was the same old earth to him wrapped in the mantle of his gloom.

But when he met along the hill a company of prophets hasting,
Striking psaltery, harp, and tabret, and the pipe's breath blowing clear,
When singing all at once they came, in wild accord their music wasting,
The mountain answering tune for tune with mystic voices hovering near,
With sweet rude clamor storming heaven, with faces rapt in holy fear,
Singing of smoke of sacrifice from altars on the hills and scars,
Singing of power that bends the blue, that holds the leashes of the stars, —

Then as the measures round him beat and left him
    thrilling to their gladness,
A flame swept up and compassed him and burned
    the withes that bound his might,
And all his strength, to music set in a swift and
    sacred madness,
Broke at his lips in prophecy and filled his dark-
    ened soul with light.
For thine, O Music! child of God, the wings that
    lift to awful height ;
The order of the universe is thine, and thine the
    flight of stars,
And the soul treads its kingly home but to the
    passion of thy bars !

WHEN FIRST YOU WENT

WHEN first you went, O desert was the day,
    The lonely day, and desert was the night,
And alien was the power that robbed from me
The white and starlike beauty of your face,
The white and starlike splendor of your soul !
Since you were all of life, I, too, had died,
Died, not as you into the larger life,
But into nothingness, had not the thought
Of your bright being led outward, as a beam
Piercing the labyrinthine gloom shows light
Somewhere existing.
             Like a golden lure
Bringing me to the open was the thought, —
For since I loved you still, you still must be,

WHEN FIRST YOU WENT

And where you were there I must follow you.
And follow, follow, follow, cried the winds,
And follow, follow, murmured all the tides,
And follow, sang the stars that wove the web
Of their white orbits far in shining space
Where Sirius with his dark companion went.
Bound in the bands of Law they ranged the deep ;
And Law, I said, means Will to utter Law;
And Will means One, indeed, to have the Will.
And having found that One shall it not be
The One Supreme of all, whose power I prove,
Whose inconceivable intelligence
Faintly divine, and who perforce must dwell
Compact of love the most supreme of all ?
Had I found God and should I not find you ?

That love supreme will never mock my search.
That thought accordant in the infinite
The great flame of your spirit will not quench.
That power embattled through the universe
Needs in all firmaments your panoply
Of stainless purity, of crystal truth,
Your sympathy that melts into the pang,
Your blazing wrath with wrong, your tenderness
To every small or suffering thing, as sweet
As purple twilight touching throbbing eyes,
Your answer to great music when it breathes
Silver and secret speech from sphere to sphere,
Your thrill before the beauty of the earth,
Your passion for the sorrow of the race !
You who in the grey waste of night awoke

IN TITIAN'S GARDEN

When clashing mill-bells frolicking in air
Called up the day, and sounded in your ear
Clank of enormous fetters that have bound
Labor in all lands ; you whose pity went
Out on the long swell where the fisherman
Slides with his shining boat-load in the dark;
You whom the versed in state-craft paused to hear,
The sullen prisoner blest, the old man loved,
The little children ran along beside ;
You who to women were the Knight of God.
Therefore as God lives, so I know do you.

And with that knowledge comes a keener joy
Than blushing, beating, folds young love about.
Again the sky burns azure, and the stars
Lean from their depths to tell me of your state.
Again the sea-line meets the line divine,
And the surge shatters in wide melody;
The half-guessed hues that the heart swells to note
Haunting the rainbow's edges lead me on ;
And all the dropping dews of summer nights
Keep measure with the music in my heart.
And still I climb where you have gone before,
Unchallenged spirit who enclosed my days
As in a jewel, walled about with light !
And far, far off, I seem to see you go
Familiar of unknown immensity,
And pass, enlarged to all the rosy vast,
And boon companion of the dawn in heaven.

THE FIRST. EDITION OF THIS BOOK
CONSISTS OF FIVE HUNDRED COPIES
PRINTED BY JOHN WILSON AND
SON, AT THE UNIVERSITY PRESS
CAMBRIDGE MASSACHUSETTS DUR-
ING MAY M DCCC XCVII

www.ingramcontent.com/pod-product-compliance
Lightning Source LLC
Chambersburg PA
CBHW030536270326
41927CB00008B/1407